Groundwood Books / House of Anansi Press
groundwoodbooks.com

We gratefully acknowledge for their financial support of our publishing
program the Canada Council for the Arts, the Ontario Arts Council and
the Government of Canada.

Canada Council   Conseil des Arts
for the Arts   du Canada

ONTARIO ARTS COUNCIL
CONSEIL DES ARTS DE L'ONTARIO
an Ontario government agency
un organisme du gouvernement de l'Ontario

With the participation of the Government of Canada
Avec la participation du gouvernement du Canada | Canadä

Library and Archives Canada Cataloguing in Publication
Title: A forest in the city / Andrea Curtis ; illustrated by Pierre Pratt.
Names: Curtis, Andrea, author. | Pratt, Pierre, illustrator.
Description: Series statement: ThinkCities 1
Identifiers: Canadiana (print) 20190146540 | Canadiana (ebook)
   20190146567 | ISBN 9781773061429 (hardcover) | ISBN
   9781773061436 (EPUB) | ISBN 9781773063522 (Kindle)
Subjects: LCSH: Urban forestry—Juvenile literature. | LCSH: Trees in
   cities—Juvenile literature. | LCSH: Urban ecology (Sociology)—Juvenile
   literature. | LCSH: Forest ecology—Juvenile literature.
Classification: LCC SB436 .C87 2020 | DDC j635.9/77—dc23

The illustrations were created in gouache on paper.
Design by Michael Solomon
Printed and bound in Malaysia

MIX
Paper from
responsible sources
FSC FSC® C012700
www.fsc.org

For my city neighbors, whose
kindness runs as deep as the roots of
our shared trees. — AC

A FOREST
IN THE CITY

ANDREA CURTIS

ILLUSTRATED BY
PIERRE PRATT

Groundwood Books
House of Anansi Press
Toronto   Berkeley

Imagine a city draped in a blanket of green. A place where trees lean over sidewalks, lending shade to people and other creatures. Where the air is cool and clean, where the trundle of streetcars and the sound of honking horns are muffled by the leaves and branches.

Imagine a busy, humming city with a lush canopy of leaves making everyone down below feel safe, calm and connected to the earth.

Is this the city you know?

5

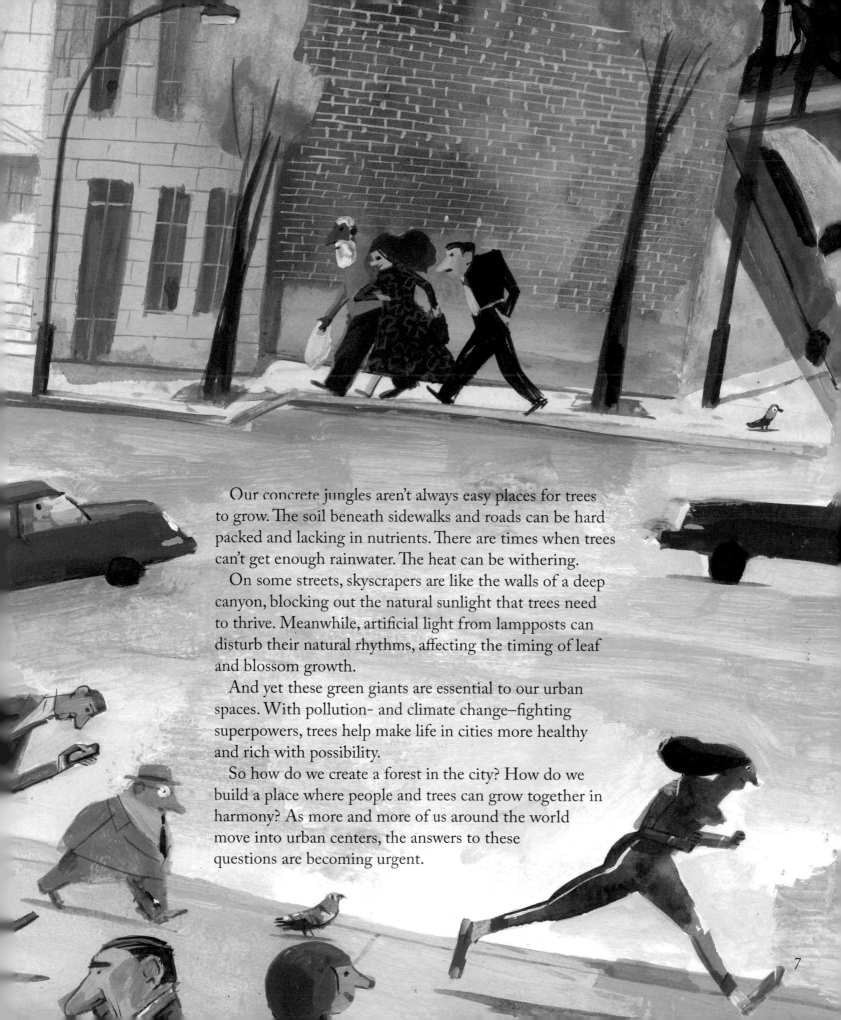

Our concrete jungles aren't always easy places for trees to grow. The soil beneath sidewalks and roads can be hard packed and lacking in nutrients. There are times when trees can't get enough rainwater. The heat can be withering.

On some streets, skyscrapers are like the walls of a deep canyon, blocking out the natural sunlight that trees need to thrive. Meanwhile, artificial light from lampposts can disturb their natural rhythms, affecting the timing of leaf and blossom growth.

And yet these green giants are essential to our urban spaces. With pollution- and climate change–fighting superpowers, trees help make life in cities more healthy and rich with possibility.

So how do we create a forest in the city? How do we build a place where people and trees can grow together in harmony? As more and more of us around the world move into urban centers, the answers to these questions are becoming urgent.

Trees have many stories to tell. They have helped shape the history and growth of cities around the world.

But before there were cities at all, the First Peoples carved homes from the forests and green spaces near the rivers, lakes, streams and oceans where they lived. They had a deep connection to the land and the trees.

As new people arrived, sometimes from far away, they cut down the trees and dug up the roots to make way for more homes and paths, then roads and buildings. They built houses and furniture and made tools. They burned the wood to cook their food and warm themselves.

Some trees continued to grow near the outskirts of these early cities or in woodlots that were accessible to everyone. A few were left near churches, temples, mosques or by the city walls where people gathered to celebrate or to sell goods on market day. Wealthy people cultivated trees in their private walled gardens.

It wasn't until about four hundred years ago that Western cities began planting trees that everyone could enjoy along a few main roads or parade routes. Even then, most places did not have a lot of trees or shrubs in their dense central cores.

Then, in the late 1700s, industrialization began. Societies moved from an economy based on growing things on the land to one relying on manufacturing goods. Once factories that could mass-produce everything from clothing to farm implements moved into the cities, urban populations exploded.

These crowded places were often dirty and polluted. Public spaces such as New York's Central Park and London's Victoria Park were created so that city dwellers could enjoy clean air and the healing power of trees and nature. Such parks were so well used that it soon became common for cities to plan for and plant trees in parks and along streets.

Shortly after the First World War (1914-1918), a deadly fungus spread by the elm bark beetle began killing many of the majestic elm trees arching over streets and sidewalks in Britain and Europe.

Within twenty years, Dutch elm disease had traveled to Asia and North America, killing hundreds of thousands of trees over several decades. The disease devastated many places, leaving them looking barren and, in some cases, struggling with air- and water-quality issues.

It wasn't until the trees were gone that people began to truly understand how important they are to cities.

In the 1960s, University of Toronto professor Erik Jorgensen coined the term "urban forest." He and others wanted to emphasize that trees in the city should be treated differently from those in traditional forests. They need to be understood as part of a unique, interconnected ecosystem that plays an essential role in urban life.

Dig down deep into the soil below the streets and
sidewalks. This is where a healthy urban forest begins.

A tree's roots are its anchor, making it stable and strong.
The roots suck up water and nutrients from the soil so the
tree can grow. A healthy root system can spread out far
wider underground than the tree's widest branches above
and may reach down about three feet (one meter) deep.

Trees communicate with each other through their root
systems — their own social network, which scientists call
the Wood Wide Web. Certain kinds of common fungi
in the soil weave through the tips of tree roots, creating

a connected community of organisms that support water absorption, the sharing of nutrients and even information — such as the existence of a toxic plant growing in the same environment.

That root system also helps build up the soil below the streets and buildings, preventing it from washing away in heavy rains. By drinking up rainfall or melting snow, the soil and root matter also slows excess runoff from storms that can overwhelm lakes and rivers with pollution or even cause a flood.

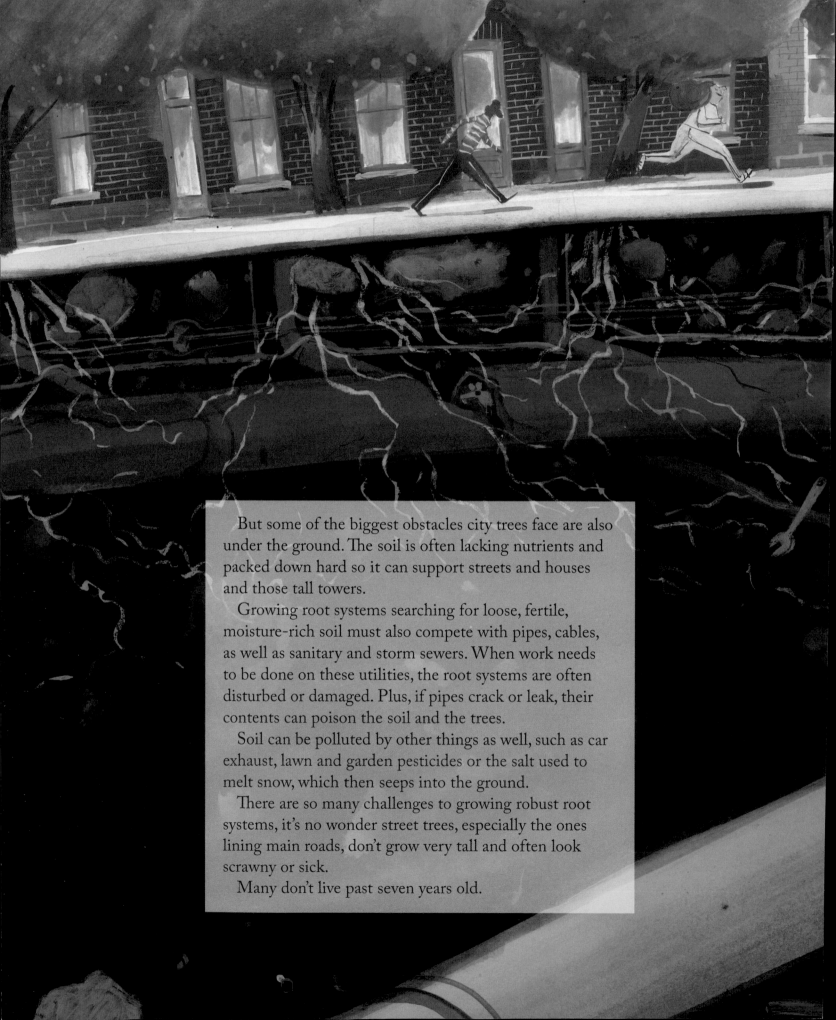

But some of the biggest obstacles city trees face are also under the ground. The soil is often lacking nutrients and packed down hard so it can support streets and houses and those tall towers.

Growing root systems searching for loose, fertile, moisture-rich soil must also compete with pipes, cables, as well as sanitary and storm sewers. When work needs to be done on these utilities, the root systems are often disturbed or damaged. Plus, if pipes crack or leak, their contents can poison the soil and the trees.

Soil can be polluted by other things as well, such as car exhaust, lawn and garden pesticides or the salt used to melt snow, which then seeps into the ground.

There are so many challenges to growing robust root systems, it's no wonder street trees, especially the ones lining main roads, don't grow very tall and often look scrawny or sick.

Many don't live past seven years old.

A large mature tree planted on its own needs more than one thousand cubic feet (thirty cubic meters) of good fertile soil to grow big and strong. That's enough to fill three dump trucks!

Of course, on streets where there are lots of buildings, with pavement above ground and utilities underneath, there's not always enough soil. So urban foresters look for ways to help trees make the most of the limited growing space.

Choosing the right tree for the site, planting it properly and providing good soil are key to improving life expectancy. Trees that are native to a particular location, for example, tend to be better adapted to the local climate. Or a certain tree species might be known for its tolerance of dry conditions or sandy soil. Easy-growing shrubs can also beautify those crowded streets where there's simply not enough soil for large trees to survive to maturity.

Urban foresters also try to help city trees by designing better growing spaces for them.

On main thoroughfares in Toronto, you might see several trees planted in long continuous soil trenches where the roots can stretch out. Some street trees in Winnipeg and other cities are placed in planters raised off the sidewalk so the soil is protected from compaction. Lots of cities also use specially formulated "structural soil" — a mixture of crushed stones and clay loam — that provides breathing space for tree roots to expand.

Suspended concrete sidewalks are used in cities from Boston to Charlotte, North Carolina. Metal or concrete posts dug deep into the earth provide support so the weight of the pavement can be suspended overtop like a platform, and the sidewalk doesn't press on the soil.

Underneath the north plaza at New York City's famous Lincoln Center, large plastic frames called soil cells were installed above an underground parking garage. These soil cells prevent soil compaction and ensure adequate growing space for the London plane trees that shade visitors to the site.

Below our streets, sidewalks and yards, thirsty tree roots are always searching for moisture and nutrients.

Homeowners sometimes complain that these roots are responsible for damage to water and sewer lines or the foundations of their houses. The same goes for public sidewalks and roads. Trees are blamed for lifting them up or causing cracks.

On some city streets you might even see roots emerging from the sidewalk like a many-armed creature trying to escape the earth.

In Los Angeles, cracked and lifted pavement over growing roots became such a hazard that lawyers for people with disabilities sued the city. In a landmark settlement, the city committed to spend more than a billion dollars to fix the huge repair backlog.

But trees aren't the cause of these problems. Rather, poor planning, planting and maintenance as well as aging roads, sidewalks, foundations and pipes are the reasons.

Trees, like many of the huge ficus in Los Angeles, were often planted too close to roads or sidewalks, with little thought to how big they would eventually grow. If trees in such close quarters aren't carefully maintained, moisture- and nutrient-seeking roots will take advantage of cracks and grow into the space.

Changing weather — like the cycle of freeze and thaw in northern cities — can also shift cement or concrete, causing gaps and breaks. If there's enough moisture and soil available, resourceful tree roots will seek out these spots.

Tree roots aren't strong enough to crack cement or pipes on their own, but they will take advantage if given a chance!

19

Tunnel up inside a tree, where layers of cells form
the trunk. Next to the heartwood, which is the central
supporting layer of the tree, is the sapwood. This layer is
a kind of giant pump, drawing nutrient-filled water from
the roots into the branches and leaves.

The cambium is next. It is a thin layer of growing tissue
and the reason trees expand in diameter every year.

The inner bark, or phloem, acts like a food supply line,
transporting sap (sugars and other nutrients produced by
the leaves) to feed the rest of the tree.

The bark is the tough outside layer made of dead tissue.
It insulates and protects the inside, like our skin protects
internal organs or a shell protects a snail.

Cambium
Phloem
Bark

Heartwood   Sapwood

If there's enough moisture in the air, moss and colorful lichens will grow on the bark. These plants don't harm the urban forest. In fact, they can help find air pollution hot spots. Scientists from Portland, Oregon, to Cordóba, Argentina, monitor air quality by mapping lichens and mosses on city trees, testing samples for contaminants.

But just like our skin and a snail's shell, bark can be damaged, especially when it's young and tender. If the damage is serious, the tree's growth can be slowed or the tree can become sick and even die.

As trees grow taller and their trunks wider, the bark becomes thick and tough.

But sometimes even that can't stop diseases and harmful insects.

21

Most bugs are beneficial to trees. Some, like bees, pollinate trees and other flowering plants, making sure they reproduce. Others, like ladybugs, are predators, killing and eating insects that can be harmful.

But there are also very destructive pests that threaten the health and future of the urban forest.

Some harmful insects have arrived from far away — hitchhiking in large shipping containers or in products brought in through international trade — despite rules and regulations to stop them. These insects are called invasive species and they can get out of control quickly because they have no natural predators in their new environment.

Some, like the emerald ash borer, dig holes in the bark, lay eggs, then the larvae feed beneath it (see cutaway view at right). Others eat only the leaves. Insects such as the Asian longhorned beetle, which attacks many species in North America, tunnel into the trunk.

Native insect species — the kind that have been around for a long time — are usually not dangerous to the urban

forest because they are kept in check by natural predators. But changes in our climate, especially drought conditions or extreme heat, are altering ecosystems. This puts stress on the urban forest and makes it more vulnerable to both native and invasive insects.

Cities such as Toronto and Chicago face the additional problem of having planted too many trees of one or two species many years ago. If a pest attacks that type of tree — as the elm bark beetle has done — significant parts of the urban forest can be at risk.

Scientists have devised many ways to stop or slow these pests, including removing the insects' eggs and introducing natural insect enemies such as parasitic wasps.

If the infestation is severe, insecticides may be used to kill the bugs or disease. Foresters will also identify and remove infected trees one by one.

But when it comes to invasive species, the best solution is prevention. Cities need to plant a diverse variety of tree species to protect against loss, as well as stop pests from getting into the urban forest in the first place.

24

Tree trunks can also be damaged by you and me. That's why most cities have rules against attaching signs to trees, removing bark or otherwise harming them.

Municipalities often erect small fences, cages or grates around trees. Some are temporary and made of plastic or metal. But others are colorful and whimsical, designed to delight and inspire, as well as shield the trees from harm.

Raised seating or shrub and flower beds can also help protect trunks from car doors or garbage pickup, or from being injured by bicycle locks or the burn of dog pee.

Occasionally, a cage or grate is placed too close to the trunk and there's not enough room for growth. These trees can become stunted and die.

But some trees manage to adapt to their environment, no matter how restricted.

Search around and you might see trees that seem to have magically grown through fences, or even appear to be gobbling up street signs, bicycles and mailboxes!

25

Look up, up, up. High in the canopy is where trees wage their toughest fight of all — not against bugs or disease or wires, but against climate change.

Carbon dioxide (CO_2) is a gas that is released as a result of human activities such as deforestation and burning fossil fuels like oil or coal to run our cars, factories and homes. Our society produces too much CO_2, and it is one of the reasons our planet is warming and the climate is changing.

Trees can help. Their leaves absorb this gas and act like a natural air purifier. Through a process called photosynthesis, the trees use the energy of the sun to turn water and CO_2 into their own food, as well as oxygen for the rest of us to breathe.

The bigger, healthier and older the tree, the more carbon dioxide it absorbs and the more oxygen it can produce. That's one of the reasons it's so important to plan for and create space for large trees in the city.

Every day, a single mature tree between forty to seventy feet (twelve to twenty-one meters) tall can provide four people with enough oxygen to breathe.

Tree leaves also fight climate change and improve people's health by capturing and trapping dirt and other chemicals from the air, reducing pollution in our cities.

Trees can make the city cooler, as well. Researchers call urban centers "heat islands" because all the hard surfaces — like pavement and buildings — soak up the sun's hot rays. But tree leaves reflect and drink in the sun before it has a chance to heat up the ground. They also add moisture to the air and create shade.

In fact, trees shading the sunny side of a building can reduce air-conditioning use by up to 30 percent.

It's not easy to put a dollar value on the beauty, comfort and pleasure that trees provide. But there are some benefits of the urban forest — like fighting climate change, improving people's mental and physical health, and cutting down on energy use — that can save tens of millions of dollars a year in each city. The savings jump up to five hundred million dollars a year in megacities such as Beijing and Buenos Aires.

In the same way that people need regular checkups with a doctor to stay healthy, trees in the city require ongoing care and maintenance. No wonder some of the people who take care of the urban forest are known as tree surgeons!

Looking after trees growing on private property is the responsibility of the home or business owner. When trees are young, they must be watered regularly. As they age, branches should be pruned to encourage good health and a species' natural shape. If a tree is not well formed — too many branches on one side, for instance — it will be more vulnerable to wind and storm damage.

When a tree becomes sick or old and must be cut down, professionals are usually called in. They sometimes have to use cranes and heavy machinery. It can be dangerous and expensive to remove a big tree from a small city yard.

Trees on public land, like those beside many sidewalks

and roads, in parks and in front of public buildings, are usually tended by city workers. They prune branches to ensure the tree remains healthy and doesn't interfere with power lines, streetlights or traffic signs. They water young trees and leave mulch around the base so the soil stays moist down below. City workers also manage insects or diseases and remove sick or dead trees.

In certain parks and urban nature areas, such as High Park in Toronto, urban foresters deliberately set small controlled fires called prescribed burns. Intended to restore and protect the park ecosystem, the fire is managed very carefully so it burns close to the ground, consuming only twigs, grasses and dry leaves.

Prescribed burns imitate the many small natural fires that occur regularly in traditional forests. These ecosystems actually grow more vigorously after a fire.

Pull back the leaves, peer into the branches and you will find a whole world of living things — from insects to birds, squirrels to raccoons. If you are very, very quiet you might even see the flicker of a fox's tail down around the trunk, a rabbit ducking beneath a low-hanging branch or a deer stopping to nibble on tender new shoots.

City trees are the home and habitat of many different creatures. They provide shelter, nesting areas, hiding places, and food from their flowers, nuts, seeds, berries, leaves and woody parts.

Lots of people also enjoy the bounty of city trees. Medicines to help with everything from headaches to sore throats are made from the bark, leaves and buds of species such as balsam fir and willow. Furniture, flooring and tools can be constructed from the wood. Dead leaves

collected by city dwellers can be turned into rich compost that will help grow new gardens, food and trees.

Depending on their location and climate, cities can also grow pretty much any variety of tree fruit, including apples, pears, plums and cherries. Nuts such as hazelnuts, chestnuts and walnuts grow in the urban forest, too. It is even possible to tap city trees to collect sap and make tasty syrups.

Sometimes fruit rots or falls to the sidewalk and goes to waste. But in cities from Ottawa to Seattle, gleaners are coming together to pick fruit and nuts. They share the edibles among themselves and the owner of the tree, or donate them to people and organizations that may not have access to fresh, locally grown food.

33

Unfortunately, not everyone loves our city trees.

Branches can fall and crush cars or houses or bring
down electrical wires. Nuts and seeds, fruit or flowers
might have a funky smell or fall and leave a mess. Trees
can be the home of noisy birds and prowling animals that
love to root around in our garbage cans.

There are people who say they just prefer a wide stretch
of green grass to a wide tree canopy. Others are allergic.
The pollen of certain tree species makes their eyes and
throat itchy and sore.

Caring for city trees on private land can also be
challenging because there are many rules and regulations
intended to protect them. Even though a tree is on your
property, you may still have to ask the city's permission to
prune it or cut it down.

Conflict between neighbors occasionally erupts over trees. Maybe one person likes shade, and the other prefers sun. They might argue over who rakes up the leaves or how to trim overhanging branches or what to do when their view is blocked. One woman in Vancouver went so far as to poison city trees that she felt were ruining her view of the ocean and mountains.

Yet trees are an essential ingredient in our shared urban experience. They help us both individually and as a community.

Living together in cities, we always have to weigh what is important to us as individuals, what is important to the collective good and, especially, how we might find a balance that works for everyone.

Glance up past the knobbly trunk, through the wide branches and leaves of a city tree, and you might see puzzle pieces of blue sky. You might glimpse a bird bringing worms to its young or a squirrel gathering nuts for the winter.

The urban forest is a complex ecosystem, a web of intimate connections, and you are part of it. We must all take care of the trees, for they offer us so much in return.

Just having a view of trees has been shown to help people recovering from surgery, decrease rates of depression and stress, and simply make people happier.

When those living in apartment buildings have treed spaces nearby, they report deeper connections to one another.

A thriving urban forest can even lower crime rates. Researchers speculate it's because treed areas attract more people and suggest to others that the neighbors care about their environment.

Trees also improve road safety, because the streets appear narrower and drivers go more slowly.

City trees aren't just pretty ornaments. They are necessities that enrich and sustain our lives.

Imagine a city draped in a blanket of green.

This can be the city you know.

Our actions have a direct impact on the health of the environment and the urban forest. Now is the time to get involved. Recovering the canopy once it's lost can take seventy-five to one hundred years.

As citizens, we need to push for and support decisions that prioritize the well-being of our urban forest. We can all make a difference — tree by tree. In fact, it's up to us to make sure the urban forest flourishes. Our future in cities may depend on it.

What can we do to help the urban forest?

- Encourage people in your community, school and home to plan for and plant trees where there is fertile soil and space for them to grow.
- Help water young trees after they are planted to encourage root growth.
- If you see a sick or dying tree, get it the help it needs. If the tree is on public land, call the city and ask for the Urban Forestry department.
- Inquire if you, your family or your class can adopt a tree on public land and water and maintain it to make sure it stays healthy.

the trees!

- Native species support greater biodiversity, including native insects and wildlife. Save seeds from native species in your community. Learn how to grow a tree from seed and ask permission from your school or the city to plant it.
- Start a tree festival in your neighborhood or school to celebrate city trees.
- Do a tree inventory in your area. Learn the trees' names and how to identify different species. Collect information about the size, health and location of the trees. This can help your neighborhood and city care for the trees and know when they need to be maintained or replaced. (See neighbourwoods.org for ideas and inspiration.)
- Push your city to plant trees in neighborhoods that don't have canopy cover. In some cities, researchers have shown that lower-income areas have fewer trees and, as a result, fewer of the health and environmental benefits. Trees should be for everyone.
- Advocate for decision makers in your city to make space for trees when they are planning new development or redevelopment.

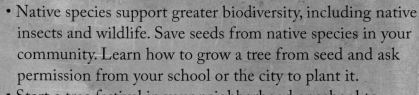

Glossary

Cambium: a thin layer of growing tissue inside the tree. Every year this tissue produces new bark and wood, causing the tree to expand in diameter.

Canopy: the uppermost layer of branches and leaves in the urban forest.

Carbon dioxide: a colorless, odorless gas that is a mixture of carbon and oxygen (CO_2). People and animals breathe it out. Whenever something organic is burned (as in gas), carbon dioxide is created. It is considered a "greenhouse gas," and it contributes to climate change.

Deforestation: the destruction or clearing of forests to make way for other uses of the land.

Ecosystem: a community of animals and plants that interact with each other and their environment.

Fossil fuels: any of a variety of fuels, such as coal, oil or natural gas, which have been formed from the remains of prehistoric plants and animals.

Gleaner: a person who collects something little by little.

Heartwood: the central supporting layer of the tree. This layer is actually dead wood, but it does not decay or lose strength.

Heat island: an urban area that is significantly warmer than surrounding rural areas as a result of human activities and human-built structures.

Insecticide: a toxic substance used to kill insects.

Invasive species: a plant, fungus or animal species that is not native to a particular area.

Mulch: a layer of mostly organic material (leaves or wood chips, for example) applied to the surface of the soil.

Native species: a species of plant, fungus or animal that normally lives and thrives in a particular ecosystem.

Nutrient: something that is needed by people, animals and plants to stay strong and healthy, such as proteins, minerals and vitamins.

Organic matter: natural matter, such as decaying leaves or wood, that has come from a recently living organism.

Organism: a living plant or animal.

Phloem: the inner-bark layer of a tree, which acts like a food supply line, transporting sap (sugars and other nutrients produced by the leaves) to feed the rest of the organism.

Photosynthesis: a chemical process by which green plants use water, sunlight and carbon dioxide (CO_2) to make their food and release oxygen into the air.

Prescribed burn: a small, controlled fire that is deliberately set by professional foresters in order to restore and protect a particular ecosystem. The fire is managed in such a way that it burns only dry leaves, twigs and grasses, but does not hurt larger trees.

Pruning: the act of cutting branches from a tree or bush to make it grow more strongly.

Runoff: the draining away of water (and the substances in it, such as soil) from the surface of land or built structures.

Sapwood: one of the outer layers of new wood inside a tree. It acts like a pump, drawing nutrient-filled water from the roots into the branches and leaves. Also known as xylem.

Seedling: a young plant grown from seed.

Soil cell: an artificial structure designed to be filled with planting soil to encourage strong tree roots, stormwater management and pavement support.

Structural soil: an artificially created growing medium that is a mixture of crushed stone, clay loam and other substances intended to provide stability for pavement and also space for root growth.

Tree nursery: a place where trees are planted, grown and cared for.

Selected Sources

Many sources were used to research this book. Students and teachers will find the following sites useful for further reading.

Trees
arborday.org
hungrytrees.com (for fun!)
naturewithin.info
notfarfromthetree.org
oufc.org
treecanada.ca

Cities
citylab.com
nextcity.org

Climate change
climate.nasa.gov
science.howstuffworks.com/environmental

Invasive insect species
invasivespeciescentre.ca

These books offer insight and additional research possibilities for older readers.

Haskell, David George. *The Songs of Trees: Stories from Nature's Great Connectors*. Viking, 2017.

Lawrence, Henry W. *City Trees: A Historical Geography from the Renaissance through the Nineteenth Century*. University of Virginia Press, 2006.

Wohlleben, Peter. *The Hidden Life of Trees: What They Feel, How They Communicate. Discoveries from a Secret World*. Greystone Books, 2015. (Younger readers will be interested in Wohlleben's kids' version, *Can You Hear the Trees Talking?: Discovering the Hidden Life of the Forest*, Greystone Kids, 2019.)

Acknowledgments

Many thanks for the time and insights of Professor Danijela Puric-Mladenovic at the University of Toronto's Faculty of Forestry. Deep gratitude also to Nan Froman, Emma Sakamoto, illustrator Pierre Pratt, art director Michael Solomon, and the other good people of Groundwood, especially the late Sheila Barry, whose kindness, wisdom and sense of fun made everything seem possible.